The Martyred Madonna

— The —
Martyred Madonna

Elizabeth Heidelsen

"SS = Schutzstaffel"

authorHOUSE

AuthorHouse™
1663 Liberty Drive
Bloomington, IN 47403
www.authorhouse.com
Phone: 1 (800) 839-8640

© 2014 Elizabeth Heidelsen. All rights reserved.

No part of this book may be reproduced, stored in a retrieval system, or transmitted by any means without the written permission of the author.

Published by AuthorHouse 04/13/2017

Library of Congress Control Number: 2014910096

ISBN: 978-1-4969-1746-1 (sc)
ISBN: 978-1-4969-1745-4 (e)

Print information available on the last page.

Any people depicted in stock imagery provided by Thinkstock are models, and such images are being used for illustrative purposes only. Certain stock imagery © Thinkstock.

This book is printed on acid-free paper.

Because of the dynamic nature of the Internet, any web addresses or links contained in this book may have changed since publication and may no longer be valid. The views expressed in this work are solely those of the author and do not necessarily reflect the views of the publisher, and the publisher hereby disclaims any responsibility for them.

Contents

The Inaudible Cry—.. 1
Charitable Wolves In Sheep's Clothing:................................. 4
Children's Charity Code of Conduct:..................................... 9
"Weighing the Effectiveness of Charities"............................ 12
Aberration of Nature's Parenting—
The Unnatural Breaking of the Emotional Womb:............. 16
Child Abuse 'Prevention' History:....................................... 23
The 'Lucifer Effect' In Society 28
The Modernized Nativity: 33
English Lambchops =... 39
Lost Lambs' Post-Separation Depression— 48
"The Tears of Madonna: Adoption or Abduction?".............. 50

Bibliography:.. 55

Dedicated to
the Madonnas &
their precious Lambs
in dire need of
Civil Rights defense
against the organized forces
of the modern day
Schuttzstaffel.

= SS = Social
Services

*

In honorable
devotion
to the
Heavenly
Madonna
&
Her
Lamb of God.

*

To My Cherished Son & Daughter
Syd & Elizabeth

In Defense of Our Family.

*

The Inaudible Cry—

Of all creatures in nature, the lamb is most candidly representative of humility & the epitome of vulnerability to the wolves of the pasture; in symbolic reference, lambs throughout history have been identified with the essence of purity & unblemished innocence as the Hebrew insignia written in blood above the doors of Jews during the Passover.

As the voice of a lamb can be heard crying out blinded from visibility behind a field of towering grain, he can still be found amongst the growth in the midst of his confusion due to this audible cry. In analogy, the misfortunate human child victimized by governmental child 'protection' services is comparable to this innocent lamb—abandoned by society & forced into estrangement from the related parents whom were by nature intended to comfort & nurture them; however, this human child's cry is made mercilessly *inaudible* due to the stifling of hard-hearted 'advocates' of child charity organizations, the chaotic snuffing of the media &/or press, & the silencing of apathetic onlookers of the acknowledged wrongdoings of relentless occurring.

These innocent lambs' cries are being stifled to the point of oppressive emotional suffering ultimately rendered as clinical depression, imploded as somatic symptoms of subsequent real physical ailments, & surfacing spontaneously through aggressive tantrums & violence-inducing anger; if left unresolved, the lambs gain a 'helpless' mentality once they learn of their mother's unwillingness to respond to the cries of their deep-seated grief from abandonment. The likelihood of intense morbidity & early mortality are the resultant extent of procured, prolonged anguish & suffering.

Again, these children aren't merely crying, but wailing in emotional pain from the *forced* abandonment from their parents, the government-encouraged rejection from other family members, & the complete silence they receive in return for not having their mothers respond to their cries of distress. With no consolation returned for their incessant crying, these children forced into abandonment become engrossed with bitterness, resentment, & hatred of others.

According to research, children's physical proximity to their respective parent(s) is directly related to overall increased health effects including multiple short-term & long-term results; among these are a mother's quicker responses to a child's cries allowing for increased sense of safety & well-being, a higher emotional intelligent quotient being apparent with toddler co-napping, intellectual stimulation being heightened from more intense stimulation, and parental consistency being interpreted as emotional reassurance. These children who are uninterrupted with contact & communication with parents are more readily equipped to grow into confident, stable adults.

On the other hand, those children (denied their basic civil rights to live as a free citizen) are comparably prisoners of war within their own country's 'protective' services. Under strict enforcement by county government officials, children are demanded to no longer speak to their own mothers & fathers without reassurance & comfort during this 'hostage' period.

To the misfortune of the majority of these children, this 'hostage' period not only suggests, but demands that their Constitutional right to freedom of speech is denied. This denial is equivalently comparable to the overbearing control that a slave is placed under – being ordered as to what, to whom, & when they can or can't communicate. Although these 'hostage' periods can last a few months to a few years, some CPS (Child Protection Services) 'cases' result in the permanence of estrangement from the child's birth family. There is no time period during which the child or correlating parental figures are offered respect, reconciliation, or monetary restitution for having had his or her child stolen needlessly; nor for the intense emotional anguish & prolonged mental infliction suffered is there any apology of inconsideration or courteous acknowledgement of improper treatment. The opposite quite regularly occurs with the local police force (city & sheriff) along with neighboring counties bonding together to falsify documentation in support of deceptive trickery in ultimate thievery of vulnerable parents' children. Many times, the women are placed under false arrest, subsequent illegal imprisonment, held in isolation while incarcerated, & left with law enforcement 'branding' which surfaces during required employment & housing background checks. Just as significant to mention is the lack of reprimanding that occurs with these government workers; furthermore, if a parent aims to defend his or herself, often times back-lashing from policemen & social workers only intensifies with continual slander & intentional misrepresentation against the parent being 'unfit.'

Reviewing history's findings of government forces overtaking parental rights with degrading harassment, the S.S. initials which currently represents Social Services is the same acronym utilized less than 100 years ago for the Schutzstaffel social employees under Hitler's dictatorial authority. As German supremacists set the stage for depleting humans of their rights & dignity, Hitler believed the "Ubermensch" & "Unterfrauen" of fair physical characteristics to be the only respectable race during his expected 1,000 year reign of the Nazis. With abduction of children for the breeding of a 'perfect' species, forced adoptions were instigated under government control.

In 1932, the initiation of the Lebensborn program created centers in Germany for the intent of breeding targeted, 'perfect' infants of forced adoption; references estimate approximately 200,000 blonde hair, blue-eyed children were abducted from Polish parents by the German forces. Originally known as the German warrior tribes of the Aryan, this taller blonde hair, green or blue eyed individual enveloped the Nazi racial criteria of Hitler's dictatorship; as mentioned, women & children of Poland were permanently abducted while the Norwegian countries' height & apparent look were also of specific targeting for recreation.

These Lebensborn children were denied complete access to parental communication & were convinced under protocol that their parents had rejected them; exemplary evidence of such protocol are specific accounts of SS nurses deliberately persuading children that their Lebensborn presence was the result of parental abandonment. Ironically, these children were at a later age beaten if refusing Nazi education; tragically, most were transferred to concentration camps back in Poland to be killed. Only the remainder of these children that barely escaped the tormenting of Hitler's officials was adopted into SS families.

Charitable Wolves In Sheep's Clothing:

With unnecessary adoptions being a reoccurring historical occurrence, ironically, 'Christian, faith-based' organizations are also targeting these children as victims of faked abuse to grow their illegal funding. Children, as most Judeo-Christians acknowledge, are considered the essence of heaven itself with the recording of men begetting men detailed in the holy acclaimed Scriptures of the Old Testament; yet, these denominational Christian charities are utilized by the State's circulated Federal money to drive the 'royal essence' of Adam's descendants into the outward perception of stigmatic ruin in the poverty of chronic, life-long implication.

One must question the ethical standard of the Christ-fearing, Church-based charities which knowingly & with driven intent distinctively scorn these 'royal descendants' as unworthy of attentive acceptance from their own families. In regards to the normalcy of ethical integrity whether of secular or non-secular origin, there is a definitive argument towards the allowance of these organizations to continue their 'faith-entrusted' & tithing-supported 'acts of God's mercy' when knowingly fit, willing, & safe parents are having their children intentionally stolen from them by the employees of these charitable institutions.

Reminding these charitable forces of their purpose to protect children rather than abduct them is similarly a slap on the wrist of these criminals. These charity-based institutions, supplying targeted children for their 'homes,' are through identified witness known to scorn their clients with words of contempt & intentional slander.

Upon entering the building of the charitable 'angels' one will see how intently negligent & indifferent their employees are towards reunifying parents with their children. The States request their 'services' in abducting children in effort to cover up for their criminal behavior. By associating themselves with a non-profit, faith-based encompassing organization, the criminals of the juvenile court shield their reputation from potential infamy of being recognized as a prostitution ring for human trafficking. For who would question the intentions & the motives of a 'Christ-based' charity that pictures impoverished, crying children on its pamphlet cover? As one reads the mission of these organizations, many state their cause similar to the following:

"In the love of Christ, we aim to protect children from the suffering & neglect of familial abuse. As angels of God's mercy, our goal is to become the hands & feet of our Almighty Savior in effort to fulfill the mission of Jesus Christ to serve & protect His little lambs."

In actuality, His Little Lambs are becoming human sacrifices to their altars of abduction; their ceremonies of sacrificial Lamb offerings are in their minds righteous obedience to the authority of the judge & the God-appointed juvenile court members. Their belief is that due to their masking behind God's holy white robes, they have disguised themselves from recognition as wolves in sheep's clothing. The requirement of the charity & their supportive courts is to insist that the biological parent (no matter how nurturing, loving, & supportive) is to be completely cut off from communication &/or access to their child.

With common sense obliterated, one must question, when does policy overrule obvious evidence of a mother's character as being 'fit' & the application of practicality to the allowance of parenthood?

A parent may in actuality be a public nursery worker who is characterized by her co-employees as kind, nurturing, & intensely loving of children; however, her fellow 'charity workers' will describe her as non-compliant, argumentative, & absurd in behavior. Many times, these charity 'angels' along with social workers & the police will write reports claiming their expertise involves the assumed authority to label the biological parent with specific psychological terminology—"bi-polar, delusional, schizophrenic, paranoid, or schizoid." In regards to the situation of 'abuse,' the parent's words are twisted accordingly to directly create 'demonic' behavior out of sometimes model-perfect parents.

As one enters the building of child-confiscating charity, an individual will notice the sign on the wall that states ". . . . The Kingdom of Heaven is such as these . . ." Mark 10:14. Ironically, the child is being given an opportunity to be abandoned, estranged, & forever exiled from their biological family all due to the ever-loving Christ workers insisting their pockets be filled. Must another Lamb of God be pulled out of the loving care of his mother's home & down the temple's aisle to the church altar of sacrifice? Must these Lambs of God writhe in misery as they are held hostage to the altar gagged & deafened to the voice of their parent while the sacrificial offering is prepared?

In reality, the 'sacrifice' not only involves excruciating emotional pain & unbearable rejection from forced abandonment, but the shock of rejection transforms itself at times into such intense physical suffering that resultant death consequently occurs; from being estranged & dumped into a strange environment, children are at war with their surroundings, emotions, & mind-altering confusion as resultant death is beckoning.

Intensifying the pain is the inability for small children under three years of age to communicate clearly; they are unable to speak of the loss of their parent, unable to tell the parent they are missed, & intensely angry at the unexplained loss of affection that occurs abruptly.

As the lamb's cry of tears can't communicate with words that they wish to be reunited, these children under three years are the prime target of abduction.

For when the child's emotional pain exceeds the norm that is experienced in most childhoods, these children are rendered emotionally-blocked, numbed of their senses (due to intense fear of isolation & rejection), & driven to explosive anger, implosive depression, & deep-seated feelings of mistrust. When their wailing attempts to be comforted by their real mothers are not answered, the child in shock becomes detached from the new caretaker that is present through avoidance of further potential rejection.

In one instance, there was a middle-aged female, model-parent who had her child slyly confiscated by the 'angel' forces. As her daughter got older & years passed, her daughter developed somatic & subsequent real illness which was intensified by the alienation from her real mother. The daughter of barely 6 years of age suffered from kidney damage requiring surgery which was more intensely affected from emotional heartbreak. Although her mother had complied with the charity's 'angel' forces, communication remained severely broken & the daughter nearly died during the surgical battles she ensued alone.

Similarly, other vital organs such as the heart can be affected by the traumatic loss in love's separation. This 'broken heart syndrome' is referred to by cardiologists as the mind-heart connection which apparently renders tangible, physical defects on the heart's functionality. Parents often complain of previously undiagnosed heart palpitations, cardiovascular disease, & mental ailments.

The traumatic forces of society interfering with God's nature are as real as the desire for an 'angel' member of Christ's church to adamantly tear Jesus from His mother Madonna's arms. Bearing no guilt, no shame, & no conscience, the government forces under many false 'hotline' calls expose the Lambs of God to this radical, unnecessary, & inappropriately unrighteous forced separation of God's child from his true mother.

All of the resultant destruction from these charities & the social work field is ignored due to the intended financial profit gained from the hands of philanthropists & devout church members. There is no boundary that 'separates them from the love of God;' therefore, they plot to demolish the very essence of civilized living—the family—& leave children unattended in group homes estranged from God's intended biological parent due to their brain-washed conscience that no matter how great their sin committed all is washed 'white as snow' with the blood of Jesus.

In whose name are they praying & in whose name are they stealing? Completely opposite names. For although they pray to Jesus, they steal to Lucifer giving to only their charity of self-interested gain. Under siege of mercy, mothers of bastard children are the object of the severest cardinal punishment in the church. In double standard, the fathers of bastard children can be instantly forgiven & if they choose to reject their wives & have even chosen an alternate homosexual partner, they can be considered the 'choice parent' for the Church.

With masked intent to confiscate a steady supply of philanthropy finances, the occurrence of sacrificial Lamb ceremonies is a steady demand which requires any form of rejection claimed. In heeding their Lucifer-like countenance, the secretary will abruptly respond to clients with haughty glare & proceed to disregard your worth as an individual. Similarly, the appointed charity social worker will ignore communication efforts except when necessary for completion of the sacrificial Lamb ceremony (which in government policy is referred to as termination of parental rights). Then, when communication is absolutely necessary, the employee will deride both the parent & the attending attorney with condescension; however, the mission statement of one particular charity reads as follows:

CHILDREN'S CHARITY CODE OF CONDUCT:

I. *The client has the right to the highest professional standards of treatment regarding dignity & respect in reflection of God's love & worth for the client as an individual.*

II. *The client is entitled to be informed of intentions of the services rendered.*

III. *The client has both a right to privacy & complete access to her file/subsequent individualized records obtained &/or created by the agency.*

IV. *The client has a right to know all aspects of services rendered regarding the individual's case at hand.*

V. *The client has a right to voice concern or grievance against any aspect of services rendered.*

Despite the above listed code of convicted Gospel voice, the client per identified witness is estranged from management &/or supervisors regarding any complaints &/or grievances he or she might have. With contemptuous argument from an employee, the client is refused treatment as 'God's worthy, highly valued' clientele while another employee offers complete negligence in never returning phone calls, e-mails, & intentionally hanging up before conversation initiates during required meetings conducted via telecommunication.

The key emphasis of the reference to prolonged anguish & suffering is that this phrase is preceded by the word 'procured'—which in definition is 'the acquisition through special attention & intended effort.' In the US, children whom CPS targets are not the result of unintended misfortune & lost accountability; contrarily, the children of CPS's victimization are the product of chronic, time-consuming effort in which each member of the CPS 'team' holds a vital role in approving of the initial abduction, subsequent abandonment, & cumulative permanent estrangement from his or her original family. Not only are children the ultimate target of punishment aimed at by the county's illegal scandal, but the children are rendered many times exempt of inheritance & familial acceptance due to the shame placed upon them through having entered the foster system.

Therefore, with citizens rendered as targets for punishment, the United States's CPS has been referred to as a child punishing system rather than a child protection system. With the parent(s) being classified as the enemy precluding redeemable allowance for a reasonable parent-child relationship, the child is left empty-handed to society's estrangement. The stigmatic resultant persona is evident as a significant drop in the child's self-esteem is identified & a lowered recognition in society occurs.

The punishment of stigmatic rejection prolongs well after the child ages into adulthood. The 'aging out' of these fostered children who are accustomed to being hand-held by government-funded officials throughout their life are upon age of 18 or older rendered as 'unfunded' to entitlement; thus, these adults who are the by-products of government manufacturing are dumped into the streets without regard to their well-being. Although various 'charity' organizations have attempted to claim these adult 'children' back into their funding, the majority of these aged 'youth' are in societal image lost to the worth of recognition.

According to the Fostering Connections Resource Center in the US, there were in September of 2008 approximately 463,000 children in the fostering system while an additional 29,000 children exited the system at 18 & above without a permanent family structure. According to collective research, studies indicate that the fostered alumni are at a rate of 25% likely to be exempt of a high school diploma or GED; additionally, less than 2% finished college in comparison to 23% of the general population. More than half of the youth 'aging out' fell into circumstantial homelessness with approximately one third of these becoming incarcerated at some point afterwards.

In the US, the state of California, New York, Illinois, Massachusetts, & Virginia possessed the highest number of 'aging out' youth in 2007 with California holding the highest number of fostered adults to total 5,188; the successor State of New York fell into second place at 1,506 while Illinois, Massachusetts, & Virginia ranged between 1,000 & 1,250 fostered children 'aging out.'

The point of emphasizing the fostered children as being 'aged out' into homelessness is that <u>although</u> the intention of government welfare programs is to aid our 'lambs' from being neglected & discriminatorily finding excuse to pull children from 'poorer' homes, in the majority of cases they end up right where they started – on poverty row.

"Weighing the Effectiveness of Charities"

As seen in the visible outpour of resistance to child abuse through charitable causes for awareness, there also lies the simple fact that the awareness factor must proceed actual causative action. So it seems the charitable foundation that is aimed to protect the victims they imply require alarm towards the endangering factual awareness. Yet the cause in many charitable cases never proceeds any further from step one.

This is resembled in the five "A's" which are implied as steps towards actual resolution to victims or endangerments of society. This includes the following: awareness, acknowledgement, assistance, actuality, & accountability. Unfortunately, many charities don't go beyond educational awareness; & therefore, these charities prevent the actual problem from being resolved &/or the victims from being defended. In the first two stages, *the actual victim is never assisted by the organization* & only offers the victim an educational resource from which pamphlets & statistical information are distributed. The victim is therefore in many ways 'punished' by these organizations if & when they do not clarify that they are PRIMARILY education resources & nothing further.

The following outlines the Five suggestive Steps for charity organizations to follow in order to not only produce actual resolutions, but also find accountability to continually aid victims in relief of their undesired circumstance.

Awareness-

At Step One, Awareness is recognized as having the potential for protecting the victim through personal education if & when this education assists the victims. Secondly, the Awareness step allows for other community members to become alert to the problem at hand which is otherwise unexposed to the public. Although education is assistive, lacking resources relevant to the cause may instigate the victim to stumble further into helplessness. When a charity looks as though it is the apparent 'aid' to the victim, the charity (other than education) may actually be lacking resources; & therefore, when actual 'help' could step in, it doesn't due to the awareness step hogging the stage. Counseling & group therapy can be included in this step because it usually doesn't involve actual solving of needed problems, nor any type of defense of the victim; this counseling primarily serves as an outlet for venting without further resourcefulness.

Acknowledgment-

During this second step, societal members have become educated & recognizant of a substantial problem. This recognition is beyond the acknowledgement of nearby community members, but involves a larger scale of recognition during which more supportive philanthropic attention is offered. Most of the tithing & financial support is usually spent on marketing, & if fortunate is able to gain attention through the internet & mass media on an opportune large scale.

Assistance-

At Step Three, Assistance—This step reaches beyond the basic cause of educating the victim & the public. Real results occur in which the victim is actually alleviated in undesirable circumstance. For instance, the charity has taken the extra step to provide financial relief, court advocate assistance, legal aid, &/or help with basic resources (shelter, food, clothing, & transportation). These basic necessities met in this stage are helpful, but prevention from the problem possibly reoccurring is usually not inclusive in this step.

Actuality-

Step Four is labeled as Actuality during which the 'actual' problem that causes the victimization or endangerment is being corrected. The victim's exact defect in life is surrendered to not only local community members, but to a movement of societal change. It is during this step that legislation has been altered to aid the victim &/or society has stepped in to take active involvement in reaching a changed outcome. Funding &/or resources are adequate in allowing for substantial resolution occurrence.

Accountability-

Step Five is explicitly reassuring to the donor that the actual donated money is offering assistance to relieve the victims as intended. This can be done with the charity being agreeable to offer graphs referencing outcomes & assistive results as related to charitable dollars.

In revealing the above steps' ability to not only alert the public, but resolve actual problems, the charity organizations can be prevented from being a 'cover up' charity that band-aids the real issues at hand. This could be done by allowing the charity to declare their level of assistance as one of the following: educational, assistive, or actual. If the charity organization is unable to assist the victims with resources other than counseling, group therapy, or educational references, then it should be labeled as such; in reflection, education is always the initial step that must be taken. In reference, these organizations could maintain their position of education since in many instances it must be on-going, reformative, & ever-adjusted to the change of statistics & detailed specifics regarding potential solutions. In consideration, this educational –type charity can require a considerable amount of support in effort to maintain investigators to collect evidence & consolidate statistics yearly if able. And in being labeled a primarily 'educational' charity, the public would be able to acknowledge exactly what purpose their funding was to be utilized. Funding should therefore also be limited to this type of organization in that it should not have financial support grossly exceed proper awareness of the issue.

The goal then of labeling of the charities respectively for their limitation in purpose would not only assist the victim in recovery, but keep charities accountable to their intention without misleading the public of their actual abilities to resolve societal concerns.

As in the situation of children's charities, the actual foundation of awareness through education occurs; yet instead of alleviating the child from an abusive family, many times there is only a faked abuse story that is created to permanently abduct the child from his or her natural, biological home. Many times in the US, children are taken for immature, unreasonable excuses as simplistic as not having proper housekeeping. As the dollars add up when the child is being fostered (at an approximate $6,000 per year) & the court is being rewarded for parental termination (at a proposed $4-6,000 dollars) while annually being employed for such falsification of necessary abduction, the child is being 'lost' to society with few to no relatives willing to befriend a victim of the governmental systems. For the stigma behind the governmental systems is alarmingly high rendering many 'lost' children the exclusion from familial relations, rejection from social acceptance, & not only labeled many times as impoverished, but abandoned to the image of being an indigent.

Aberration of Nature's Parenting— The Unnatural Breaking of the Emotional Womb:

—As most youth of the animal kingdom maintain the same instinctual emotional comfort in being close to their mother, so do human children.—

In effort to emphasize the early developmental attachment a child has to his or her mother, the acronym ABCLSR is utilized. The ABCLSR ('At Birth' Biological Connection & Long-term Symbiotic Relationship) of the child & his/her mother is conducive to indicating Mother Nature's intention to maintain a strong, inseparable union of a mother with her child. Although the initial fetal development of a child is already in synchrony with the mother's dietary habits, demeanor, & reassurance of voice recognition, the post-birth child is in similar well-being under the recognizant presence of the biological parent. As the fetal DNA are built upon the dictation of the core genetic structure of the two parents, the resultant children are programmed to appropriately respond both in physiological acceptance & 'emoto-intellectual' closeness with the parents.

Separation of the child from the parent not only destroys the initial pattern of stabilization through denied reassurance & emotional connectivity, but also rears the child in an emotionally numbing state which can alter the child's personality as later dysfunctional in society.

Ironically, in custody battles of 'The Biological Parent(s) Vs. The State,' the state employees will pinpoint a parent's personality as being 'disorderly' & 'unfit' for parenting. The State in this common situation is in desperation creating an excuse to permanently sever the mother-child relationship.

Unfortunately, common sense, logical support, & the least disruptive option for the child are often overlooked.

Although the burden lies upon the parent as being unfit & in dire need of reparation of the biological relationship to unify, it is the intent of the social State authorities to control & reel government financial assistance although there is no initial relational conflict in occurrence.

Child-rearing away from the child's biologically intended parent may trigger an aberration from the natural endorphin releases, homeostatic hormonal balances, & mentally inspiring charges exchanged between verbal & physical proximity of the child to the biological parents. When governmental associates demand a parent(s) be separated from the child, this forced developmental aberration from the norm resultantly increases chronic stress & emotional estrangement. Problematic concerns regarding the resultant opportunistic emotional 'infections' are not easily researched by professionals since the children's body/organs are still in development & thus more vulnerable to irreparable damages. Children's limited communicative capabilities also limit the ability for exact, reliant evidence to be collected.

Nature's calling for a parent to a child is so strong that much of the disruption that occurs inflicts profound effects on the child's emotional attachment ability. Childhood research has concocted the term Disorganized Attachment Disorder which causes the child to deny physical & emotional closeness to other individuals in effort to prevent himself from getting repeatedly hurt from abandonment. Ironically this mental health disorder's words respectively form the acronym DAD. A child missing his own father (& mother) has serious implications of a 'fight-or-flight' stress response from the separation. Similarly, this pattern of abandonment has a deep influence on the child's later years as adults; during adulthood, attempts at relationship attachment may be unsuccessful with waning stability, shallow intimacy, & avoidance of close communication. During the time period more recent to the initial separated years, the children will find themselves in a 'panic-stricken' state in which their inability to change the separation is being coped with. At this time the child will fluctuate between being 'present' & being spontaneously absent-minded with an impression of immaturity given to the foster parents.

Due to the deep emotional pain being felt from the separation, the child will many times maintain that mentality of indifference & emotional detachment which allows for subsequent noctouresis to occur. This is due to the child's response to emotional rejection during which the abandoned child is attempting to evade his own emotional conscience; the child reacts in 'closing down' the area of his mind to escape profound painful emotions of rejection. In delving into the physiology of the subconscious's controls, many children &/or adults who experience domestic violence develop asthma; the mind's deeper mental functioning is impaired by emotional shock which affects the respiratory control centers of the brain. Contrarily, with all of the intense studies conducted by child research institutes, there exist few which reflect upon the intense emotional –physiological connection in a child's well-being and that of the wrongdoing of forced separation from fit, biological parents.

According to the MN Child Defense program, the children most sought after by social council are children under the age of 5 years. Statistics speak how the most 'innocent lambs' are the most vulnerable to being stolen; national average shows that the largest number of children entering foster care have consisted of 3 to 5 year olds at 37% during the fiscal year 2010. In Illinois, the number of children in foster care from 0 to 5 years of age was 58%. Quite noticeably, these are the years during which the children are less able to voice their emotions & personal frustrations in self defense. The social systems' employees will tout that separation of a child from his or her parents is best completed during the child's youngest years (under 5); however, statistics show that these earlier years of development are a time period during which the children are most vulnerable & able to be emotionally damaged.

In recollection, children under the age of 6 are still in an 'emotional womb' that is both fragile & easily broken as is the shell of an egg; they figuratively haven't the coping skills both physically & emotionally to thrive without the intense emotional comfort of their biological mother. In essence, their mind & overall well-being are critically linked to the mothers whose womb created them. Being born with connective instincts with their natural mother, their symbiotic relationship includes recognizable aromas, shared endorphin exchanges, reactive homeostatic response, & an overall calmness from being physically present with each other.

Considering animals which have near miraculous encounters with their parents upon birth with unexplained instinctual activity, the marsupial kangaroo from the family Macropodidae (Latin for 'large foot') is a prime example of this occurrence. The kangaroo's fetal joeys upon birth will crawl from out of the womb & over a foot of distance along the outside of the mother's pouch until reaching the bottom of the pouch's safety. Most astonishingly the fetal joey is both blind & mute yet with two solitary frontal limbs the joey grasps the mother kangaroo's hair as the head is hurled back & forth across an instinctive pathway leading directly into the protective pouch. The umbilical cord remains attached until pulled free by the joeys' completed pathway from the birth canal to the pouch & also assisted by the kangaroo mother who licks along the pathway chosen for the baby joey. The red hairless joey during this arduous journey from the birth canal to the pouch varies in size from 0.2 to 0.9 inches; this is comparable to size & length ranging from as small as a rice grain to that of a honeybee.

Within this protective locale, the baby joey will attach to the mother's teat for ample nourishment allowing the fetal growth to mature unto proper size for 120 to 400 days. Once the joey has grown large enough to where the head can easily pop out, the joey will with natural curiosity tumble out of the pouch onto the surrounding ground only to return shortly to the comfort of the mother's sheltering pouch again. This instinctual comfort zone is much like that between a human mother & child who is without acknowledged effort drawn close to the biological mother's presence for emotional & physical nurturing.

This instinctual nature of the joey to remain comfortably close to the mother allows for proper growth & protection to be 'readily available.' As the animal kingdom's maternal instinct is to protect & provide for her offspring, so is the instinct of the human mother. Separation from the human mother is not only detrimental, but in many times fatal. For instance, reflect upon the joey's situational requirements for nurturing & thriving in the wild; the joey must remain in close physical contact with the mother & must also find direct nourishment from their biological parent. In specification, if the joey is forcefully removed from the maternal pouch's teat, the joey most expectedly dies since the flesh (although not attached by an umbilical cord) still requires the same direct maternal nourishment & actual physical attachment.

In considering legislation's effects upon the mind, body, & outcome of children's emotional IQs along with current & future relationship attachment ability, the Emotional Womb should be considered a significant source of demanded necessity that should not be denied. In essence, each child born as a citizen protected under the Constitution of any country honoring individual civil rights should place the right to the Emotional Womb to be a prevalent cause of insistence.

> —For the citizen at birth should not be denied his or her natural protection, reassurance, & well-being through Nature's providence.—

This Emotional Womb then from the ages of 0 – 5 years should be recognized as a dire nurturing period of development during which the separation of the mother from the child should be nearly impossible to mandate under government forces. Quite the opposite should occur with children being 'protected under law' who are forced into adoptions; rather the government authorities should utilize regulatory powers & financial resourcefulness in maintaining the biological relationship rather than severing it.

At a later age of near six years, the child is then able to communicate more readily making it a simpler task to defend themselves from the abuses of a deceiving juvenile court.

Yet under the ordinance of Mother Nature's providence, all citizens at birth should be offered the availability of parental affection & comfort. In essence, this critical stage of child development (requiring actual physiological responses exchanged during physical closeness between the parent & child) can be more specifically referred to as the 'Emoto-physical Womb' (from ages 0 – 5) — hence, encapsulating both emotional & physical well-being. Thus, the 'Emotional Womb' overlaps this early critical physical attachment stage & continues much longer from 0 – 15 years of age (resembling the time a child is still lenient upon the parent for considerable emotional support, identity empowerment, & overall reassurance).

> —Societal Recovery: The Cultic Cross—Speaking Up Against the Unspeakable—

Inevitably reporting of the abomination of the lamb slaughtering by the Child 'Punishing' Services is one step towards recovery. Yet, in contacting the US Medicare hotline, one has more potential for making a breakthrough since the majority of complaint officials find criminal ways to ignore the lower level departmental affairs no matter how lengthy or horrid the complaint. The costliness of the fraudulence is based upon severe discrimination, intentional theft, criminals 'covering' for criminals, thieves attempting to mob the vulnerable, & a vastly popular confiscation of children to the US altar of welfare sacrifice. Dollar not in exchange for dollar, but Federal dollars in exchange for a Lamb being slaughtered to the life that God intended for them filled with laughter, parental love, the serenity of being at home, & the comfort of being stable as a child who is not abandoned & tossed from family to family.

Once the average child is mercilessly thrown into the hotline criminal scandal, he or she is 'disengaged' with life & forced into the money-scheming process. This child has an average 'well-being' success rate of 4% with children no longer fairing well in school due to severe emotional abandonment, severe lost hope, & unspeakable shock.

For some deeply absurd reason, children are detestably refused 'heaven' by a popular support of citizens who desire to throw them into the pits of hell's mindset. Societal defense of children who are slaughtered to the system is extremely low with an oddity of defense only focused on <u>hiding the guilt</u> of the system.

Odd as it may be, senior citizens are however encouraged to contact 1-800-Medicare to report fraud & suspicious activity of facilities, businesses, & the likewise; this fraud reporting allows for $4.2 billion dollars to be recovered according to Medicare's notification of 2012. Amazingly, the difference in reporting confiscation of children for monetary usage is apparently making the politicians squirm with writhing embarrassment upon the discovery. Instead of being pleased to reveal the ability for your cover-ups to be exposed, the children's families are gagged, advocates fear for safety, & high-end socialites remain indifferently estranged from real problems of occurrence.

In quite opposite effect, the financial recovery tip from Medicare will not land you imprisonment for narcing, will not land you stigma of social isolation from fighting back, & will not throw your life into living Hades due to the intense societal threats to resist the exposure. Contrarily, child confiscation exposure is strangely an *intense societal taboo* although through modern day occurrence is calculated within invisible & visible legislation.

Taboo or not, motherhood is not an entitlement *ONLY* to the rich & those in society protected by surnames or clans of people. There is *NO justification* for the thievery of children from one family to provide children for another just because they can't breed their own offspring. There are plenty of children who are unwanted that parents willingly have given up; then how is it that the children who are cherished by their mothers are still stolen mercilessly?

Motherhood is indispensable no matter what way corrupters of society attempt to pull the entity down. Motherhood is sacred & desirable to the familial backbone that when destroyed creates intense, irreparable damage. Motherhood is the essence of escaped slavery for children who now live in fear that 'protective services' may show up to steal them. Motherhood is the politician of every childhood dream no matter what way legislative officials write the card.

Motherhood—the invisible Madonna who holds the heart of every child at the front of every genuine, caring church should not be replaced with a sacrificial altar where the Lamb is not only sacrificed, but souls are lost to the oblivion of a cultic cross.

In a day & age where the image of Madonna in the form of a lifeless concrete statue is still adored & cherished, how are citizens not more respectful of the living mothers around them who instead have their image broken down into a victimized state of life? The victimization of living 'madonnas' has become a source of bullying that is carried on from one authoritative branch to the other; from the police station to the social work authorities on further into the employment forces, the living 'madonnas' are left in isolation unsupported on the streets.

There couldn't be a more drastic image of hypocritical living – kneeling down to the image of one concrete Madonna (also an unwed mother bearing an illegitimate child) yet spitting & cursing with vile indignities at the next.

And who in their right mind would consider one respectful of their Creator while spitting at the image of the Mother of God?

CHILD ABUSE 'PREVENTION' HISTORY:

Regarding US legislation controlling the enforcement of child estrangement from parents, the statutes & subsequent revised statues are resourced under the individual states that each CPS child resides within; however, if a citizen or attorney is seeking legal guidance, the details of legal enforcement are not always identifiable concerning specifications. For instance, in the event a newly appointed attorney is seeking to provide legal counsel based upon the provided legislative statutes, he or she would be left to surmise the specifics of visitation rights &/or child support under guardianship placement. Concerning a citizen seeking to comparatively weigh potential outcomes of guardianship, many of the States' legislation would be absent of supportive specifications. Thus, finding guidance to make one's decisions would be of ill pursuit. A State not only denies a citizen justice in parenting when such lack of information is apparent, but also denies a citizen liberty from discrimination & deceptive legal practice through the State court systems. Whether rooted in negligence or with intent to remain inconspicuous for reason that the courts can sway court decisions with subjective discretion, the apparent 'attitude' of child legislation is that its principles of action are not worthy to gain specifications under written law. Many child law statutes under State ordinance vaguely address pertinent concerns regarding guardianship, parental communications, &/or acceptable foster parent interactions with birth parents. With legal representation having little to no reference to acknowledgement of universal state practice, parents are set up in this instance for seemingly intentional misrepresentation in the juvenile courts.

Considering substantial fiduciary benefit to the court employees listed on a CPS (child protective service) case, a child who would otherwise ethically be absent from the social services' listings would have been set into close familial guardianship. Children, who would be well-suited with direct family placement or at least taken 'out of the system' providing protection from State harassment, are according to researched documentation intentionally left as on-going cases. Considerably, the resultant draining of Federal government funding occurs with purported government acknowledgement & acceptability that jobs are being rendered under the fiscal support of child adoptive laws.

Under particular witness of an 'accused' juvenile's mother, guardian ad litem attorneys will rarely state their intent purpose of financial gain from TPR (termination of parental rights) with the alternative placement being an adoptive home; contrarily, most of the juvenile justice court constituents will deny the exchange of finances from TPR. This exact reason per juvenile mother's witness was stated by the guardian ad litem to be the reason guardianship as requested by the child's biological grandparents would 'never' be allowed by her due to the $500 to $1,000 USD each court member received for terminating parental rights.

The money the above attorney was referring to is the financial severance fee that is offered to State employees when a child is switched from foster placement into adoption under the "Fostering Connections in Success & Increasing Adoptions" act enacted in 2008; this new act led to increased adoptions through the State courts whether or not the new cases were 'faked' into the CPS system.

In the US, this monetary 'reward' received creates a figurative assembly of 'funerals' for children to their biological parents. Cumulatively, a considerable bonus per year (ranging up to $15,000) potentially could result under the termination of 15 to 20 children's rights to access their biological parents annually.

Depending on the court system's judges & team members' demeanor, the temptation to scorn & overhaul the disadvantaged in society (who cannot otherwise afford a personal attorney) could be too great to resist. To the misfortune of children across higher-structured societies in the global arena, 'protective' county-level counterparts of the government have cannibalized a system intended to provide for safety & nurturing. Rather the children have been placed as the 'innocent & vulnerable of society' sacrificed annually by the greed of ravenous wolves.

United States Child Protective Legislation Timeline—

1974—Walter Mondale authorized the passing of The Child Abuse Prevention & Treatment Act (P.L. 93-247) by President Richard Nixon

1997—President Bill Clinton's administration passed the Adoption & Safe Families Act (P.L. 105-89)

2008—George W. Bush's administration enacted Fostering Connections In Success & Increasing Adoptions Act (P.L. 110-351)

As Federal legislation continued to increase financial assistance leading to adoption of children, there was a similar increase in forced adoptions, falsified accusations, & abandoned children growing into adults with no supportive families. As US representative Jim McDermott (D-WA) reported on the foster system that "No parent I know abandons their children at age 18, and yet that is what our federal policy for foster care does." It seems apparent that the social stigma of having a grandchild, relative, or niece/nephew that has been labeled a foster child is unforgivable to many a family; the child then becomes not only forced as 'parent-less,' but also deprived of their grandparents, aunts/uncles, cousins, & extended family.

'Aging out' is a term utilized to describe foster children who by age are no longer able to be funded or sheltered under governmental legislation. Since the start of Clinton's 1997 act along with the Chafee Foster Care Independence Act (1999), there was a 64% increase in children 'aging out' of the foster system. Since the latter act was passed through, a cumulative 228,000 'aged out' foster children have been produced in the U.S. with the numbers near doubling from the 17,909 in 1999 to 29,516 children in 2008. In 2009, according to the AFCARS Report, nearly half a million children (at approximately 463,000) were placed into foster care in the U.S. There were also approximately over 80,000 children in the UK in temporary accommodations during the 2013 holiday season. Although these numbers are eye-opening, they also have a potential for being slightly misleading considering that the definition of 'homeless' in many developed countries is not synonymous to being 'without shelter.' Many families in the US may live in weekly pay residences which labels them as 'homeless.' Despite the understanding that State governments are placing unnecessary requirements & strict criteria on allowance of parenting, each case is stigmatizing the child & the respective birth parents. Ultimately, this creates a stronger stigmatic sense of rejection & societal disproval.

The entering of the Adam Walsh Act into US government legislation allowed a nation-wide registry for parents who've been 'hotlined.' This enactment adds to the stigmatization of citizens & even prohibits them from future adoptions or the fostering of other children. Whether or not a parent was found to be abusive or neglecting of their child during the initial &/or subsequent investigations (which occur following a Child Protective Abuse hotline), the parent is still 'registered' with the government as having been 'hotlined' for abuse.

Otherwise known as the Central Registry of Child Abuse & Neglect, a national registry allows for parents to be listed as permanently 'red flagged' for being a potentially incapable, unsafe parent. This allowance of a 'CAN check' for Child Abuse & Neglect is able to initiate a parent being 'punishable' although many times improperly labeled so through a 'false alarm' hotline call. Regulated under the Adam Walsh Act, this legislation is to some a façade of 'safeguarding' yet it is witnessed that each applicant for prospective adoptive or foster parenting is required to have a 'CAN check' performed before placement of a child through permissive submission of a DSS Form 3072.

Similar to false arrests which can besmirch one's FBI reports with false claims of criminal convictions, the Federal CAN Check (per attorney witness) is also stated to be permanently created upon initial abduction of one's child by the State under suspicion of child abuse & neglect whether or not one is guilty or innocent of the accusation(s). Therefore, future adoptions or fostering by the 'accused' mother or father is denied by the State due to the false claims' clarified stigmatization & labeling of being a potentially unfit parent.

Although the U.S. and other countries based on democratic or monarchial principles are intended for passive control of its citizens, they at times can surpass controlling force beyond what even some Communistic governments have set in place. For instance, in China, there has for decades been in place what is known as a 'brutal' One-Child policy enacted in 1979 which dictates that citizens must maintain one child per couple without being punished; however, in America, citizens aren't protected to even have the right to their one child making it difficult as an economically disadvantaged parent to protect their parenting right. One solitary 'fake hotline' call can strangle one's attempts to maintain a civilized life without the government stepping in to take over. The children many times get thrown to complete strangers, held under Draconian restrictions of communication with their parents, & backed up with police enforcement & faked criminal proceedings if needed. As to personal witness, one can be turned from 'mother' to instant 'criminal' with the local police claiming mental insanity & the push for prison containment with false accusations flying by left & right by the neighboring county sheriff.

In the US, pooled financial accounts are supplied by the previously listed acts' Federal funding yet maintained as fiduciary disbursements of the State's liking. As Tom Breitling (US attorney) explained on Target 22 News (in Kentucky), "Every time a child is not placed in a home, the State of Kentucky . . . loses money." Funding is obviously at the heart of the matter's disgusting practices rather than the overall well-being of the child. The wording of documentation, court proceedings, & final case opinions regarding the false claims of necessity of adoption are twisted in reference due to the ill-fitted claims, slanderous accusations, & faked occurrences. Thus, the intention of on-going court hearings & case meetings are directed not at reunification (although they claim to be), but at increasing the amount of faked evidence needed to make a parent look guilty of being abusive, negligent, or unfit. Critically, the issue of collecting procured evidence is seen as the next step in criminal protocol for forcing adoption without cause apart from biological communication & accessibility.

The 'Lucifer Effect' in Society

Phillip Zimbardo, a United States psychologist, coined the term 'lucifer effect' in his writings regarding the alteration of character that at times overtakes individuals transforming them from an angelic character to a demonic persona. In the same instance that society's overall character gradually & sometimes drastically shifts through history, it's imperative to take a detailed look at the cause of 'transformations' within culture. Some of the transformative patterns, if not identified & redirected towards a more beneficial outcome, will destroy societal foundations including the most cohesive one – the family.

'Abandonment disorder' isn't listed in the DSMV among the psychological terminology of acknowledged reference in the mental health field; however, this term 'abandonment disorder' is appropriately descriptive when assessing the ever-growing number of people in the world who upon life's pathway decide to instantaneously dump the 'other half' of their life – who is either a child, a spouse, or a long-term friend.

So it seems there is an abundance of self-centered individuals desiring to increase their financial gain through 'pimping' out their children & grandchildren with exhausting the government's accounts as faked child protective cases. This 'abandonment disorder' appears to be an increasingly popular trend. There appears to be a pattern of individuals suffering from this condition; this pattern entails possessing a compelling desire which repeatedly targets others as their prey. By instigating methods of destroying other people's image & overall well-being, the abandoners tend to revel in their folly of destruction over another human's life.

Abandonment is unduly difficult for young children to function under if the chosen target for forced adoption through State authorities. As they age, this younger generation many times exhibits characteristics such as belligerence & chemical dependency utilized to overcome the grief of lost parents in their childhood.

Is society apparently waning in emotional & familial support for children overall? The question is why? Why are people becoming so increasingly infatuated with the solitary consumption of their 'self' to the point that they are finding not only satisfaction & contentment with isolation, but intense pleasure in abducting children from family members, daughters, spouses, & many times given to complete strangers? The number of child hotline cases has nearly quadrupled in the last few years with ideal rescue calls being the minority of the total. Child 'hot-lining' is apparently the popular choice of unprovoked revenge that individuals are choosing.

Looking further into society's mental conscience, what is pushing these child thieves to be so hateful & hell-bent on another's destruction & so intentionally vengeful when not provoked?

In studies of physiological composition, are there individuals born with an inherited 'cruelty' gene (otherwise acclaimed 'bullying' chromosome) that makes them somewhat 'evil?' Or are these individuals developing an 'acquired cruelty syndrome' that is evolved over time through societal acceptances, environmental influences, & challenges to their conscience?

It appears that advanced societies have a tendency to outweigh the importance of family with material focus. Being that material resources are more readily available, the accumulation of possessions appears to be a consistent obsession that is learned. Parents, for instance, set the standard for a child's values through intended instruction. So whether or not cruelty is society-driven or an inherent trait obtained at birth, societal standards, values, & underlying tones should be addressed & habitually readdressed.

When a society begins to become 'unraveled at the seams' after reaching an accomplished level of civility, it becomes more apparent that cruelty towards the weaker societal members (such as children) is obliviously ignored. Is familial neglect the main contributing factor to increased crime, depleting morality, & degraded ethics?

When children's emotional health & physical safety are endangered by a society's own charity organizations & social departments (by masking their crimes under fraudulent documentation), a society is red flagged to have reached a culminated point of intentional *'hidden'* cruelty.

For instance, cruelty in society occurs in differing levels of acceptance for intended suffering. Such regressive stages of torment appear to proceed as follows: conspicuous throughout legislation, inconspicuous yet upheld through political approval/hidden through twisting of legislation's intent, unwritten within legislation yet acknowledged widely in culture, & unwritten in legislation yet slightly acknowledged by society.

—Structural Levels of Societal Cruelty—

<u>Unhidden Governmental Ordered & Approved Legislation</u>:

This level of societal, dictatorial cruelty is almost always initiated in protocol by a type of universal physical marking /branding of citizens in effort to control them – as seen in Adolf Hitler's commanded orders to mark citizens with numbers for Auswich recording.

Various forms of tormenting occur within this stage—such as seen under Hitler's regime with quarantining, incarcerating in pest infested quarters, & poisoning individuals with carbon monoxide/ lethal injections in Auswich's concentration camps. Mass incarceration may reach a level of overcrowding that requires relocation of the imprisoned.

Third, the cruelty creates a stringent application of specifications for physical & /or mental acceptance in effort to fall out of the 'rejected' category; with this understanding, civil rights protective clauses in this category would be completely abolished. (Exemplified in Hitler's 'perfect' breeding attempts.)

Fourth, the homo sapien is no longer seen as worthy of being acknowledged as 'human'—with feelings that can be related to, with a mindset of valuable emotions, &/or as a person worthy of not just equal respect, but any respect at all. (Exemplified in lack of medical care & denial of treatment for epidemic diseases in concentration camps.) Instead, the homo sapien is seen as a resource for usage & as an object to target for punishing.

Fifth, the individuals' religious convictions, ethical differences, & personal perspectives are not considered identifiable for exclusion from being forced into the 'controlled' group of citizens.

This overall level of cruelty has civilians under complete government control as an obsessively totalitarian government is the only 'free' entity & all citizens are dominated by detailed command. Death ensues many of the citizens under this level of cruelty with indifference from the dictatorial commandership that controls it.

Hidden Through Legislative Approval:

The next level of cruelty that ensues a society can be referred to as 'obscured yet conspicuously unacknowledged.' This is the level where upon the most innocent in society are not defended from infliction of suffering. These vulnerable counterparts of societal population include the elderly, the children, the disabled, the innocent prisoner, & the miscellaneous targets appearing defenseless. These individuals end up being submitted to cruel & unusual punishment that is unprovoked & many times unexpected. Vulnerability is of course key to being preyed upon by those in positions who claim their 'innocence' & right to being cruel for the solitary reason that they are employed under the government.

An example of this level of societal cruelty includes certain portions of Hitler's dictatorship in which soldiers wounded during the harsh winters were killed under 'top secret' orders with euthanasia & disguising death chambers as showers & bathrooms. 50,000 individuals forced into German mental institutions (between Dec 1939 & Aug 1941) died of carbon monoxide exposure.

Hidden Through Twisting of Legislative Intent:

Unfortunately, the difference between these two stages is sometimes not perceptible to the civilians in society because there are far too many government officials of higher authority unwilling to acknowledge the crimes of county courts. Many civilians in this stage may not have alerted authorities of the highest courts & organizations in order for the executive figures to be noted as acknowledging of the lesser counties' ill intent. This level of governmental affliction is when finances are the underlying intent of gain. The reward of finances outweighs the emotional health & overall well-being of the citizens. For instance, within social services, the child & subsequent biological parents' emotional needs are neglected & their mental health is intentionally abused in order for legislative funding to be received under forced adoption.

In this stage, religious convictions & altered perspectives may be acknowledged for exclusion from the 'targeted.'

* The latter two stages of progressive government-inflicted cruelty are stabilized under accountability protocols & a general application of checks & balances to equal rights of citizens. When government officials are found guilty of intentional misconduct, they are reprimanded severely by the higher authorities & treated as equals to civilians.

Yet with each of these stages of decreasing societal/governmental tormenting, the issue remains (with indifference to being a Jew, an elderly citizen, a female, or a child) of abandoned equality & lost humanity.

THE MODERNIZED NATIVITY:

As the sacred Scriptures read in the disciple verses of *Luke 2:7*—

"And she brought forth her firstborn son, and wrapped him in swaddling clothes, and laid him in a manger; because there was no room for them in the inn."

Halt! Contact Child Protective Services. Call the Child Abuse hotline.

A baby being born in a barn amongst farm animals with no prenatal care or proper birthing procedures—What are they thinking? Just as the juvenile justice department is contacted by various judgemental sources immediately in order to notify the local police enforcement that the juvenile is endangered with a poverty-stricken family, the modernized nativity would not have been enveloped with the ambience of a peaceful 'Silent' night.

In 'swaddling clothes?' This impoverished child must not have enough familial financial assistance for proper clothing, nourishment, & all of the necessities that a child of the days must have. Without hesitation, various notifications to the State government would be sentencing the Sacred Madonna & her unwed husband to the clamor of horrific accusations & subsequent societal shaming.

And so it would be in modern-day society . . . The police would arrive with a random miscellaneous excuse that must have the child's family investigated immediately! As in Mary & Joseph's situation, the event of a barn birth would justify the local police reasoning to arrive with pen & paper ready to smear their image, name, & reputation as being unfit as parents. Their Juvenile statement would read as follows:

Elizabeth Heidelsen

Cause of Action:

"Mother states she believes she is watched by strangers who state they are shepherds & wisemen. The juvenile's mother is exhibiting paranoid behavior along with potential schizophrenic claims such as hearing angels in the distance singing. The juvenile's mother leaves doors & windows open at all times of the night in stating that she is airing out the shelter where her & her alleged husband are residing at the time of arrival to scene. Juvenile's mother & father state that they have no record of proper prenatal care, physician or mid-wife delivery, & therefore, are considered incapable of caring for their infant. The child was found crying while lying in a pile of hay next to loose farm animals at the scene. When questioned, both parents state that they were unable to locate proper housing for the night due to lack of availability in local inns of the village; however, both parents appear delusional & potentially bi-polar. They may have arrived to the village due to a manic episode since their alleged 'home' is hours away. Juvenile's parents stated they arrived here in improper transportation – a donkey. Both parents are an immediate threat to the safety & well-being of the juvenile.

Action To Be Rendered:

Immediate removal of the juvenile from the biological parent's home.

And isn't that how the story unfolds portraying the very Child of God as a humble, impoverished infant of ignoble birth embellished in the declaration of humility. This particular lyrical presentation is historically remembered as proclaimed in well-known verse:

> *"Away in a manger,*
> *No crib" (Yes, No crib)... "for a bed;*
> *The little Lord Jesus,*
> *Lay down His sweet head.*
>
> *The stars in the bright sky*
> *Look down where He lay;*
> *.... The little Lord Jesus, asleep on the hay."*

The hay! With unbelievable conviction of low existence & humbled being, a child was laying not on a pillowtop, double-soft, Serta-plush mattress, but on the hay! The hay could have blinded & permanently crippled the very Lamb of God. How awfully negligent the <u>current, modern-day twisted thinking </u>would claim stake at the parenting abilities of this pure-hearted couple.

With modernized, rigid distaste & hatred for fellow citizens, the evil-minded societal ruinous would turn a most sacred, beautiful, God-fearing couple into the most hated, pitiful-at-parenting, & lame excuse for human beings that their minds could create.

One must question, when did we turn from our natural affection & respect for our neighbors & entitle ourselves to striking even the most innocent & nurturing of couples with acrimonious slander?

Bitter hatred—that which may not only destroy the most sacred, blessed union in historical reference between Madonna & her Child, but that which could also continually stigmatize the lives of the children & their subsequent parents.

The Lord's Scripture refers to these 'haters' as fools . . . .

> "He that hideth hatred with lying lips, and he that
> uttereth a slander, is a fool."
> —Proverbs 10:18

In essence, the Modernized Nativity scene would include a gossip stir of the village's condescension upon this traveling couple. The reproach would have included the governmental services' officers arriving on horse to condemn the relationship that changed the world's stronghold. There would be no ambience of a starry night of solitude as the harmonious relationship of nature's choice would be destroyed; the officers would arrive to stake their claim on the most celebrated night of all history. The investigative 'team' would complete their false claims of insanity upon the Mother of God, Joseph would be potentially incarcerated upon further false allegations of abuse, & once the forms were completed with their slanderous comments, the juvenile of Jesus Christ himself would disappear into the night into the hands of the over-pressing government forces that be.

And there would be the empty manger.

In the stable, there would only be Jesus' mother wailing out to the heavens in complete disarray as the forced abandonment would be seemingly unbearable upon the mind love-stricken for her Child. As enacted upon the biological parents, there would no longer be a Child to hold & love when their own mental sanity was being unrightfully questioned. Just as many parents are so devastated by the absolute ruin felt by the children being stolen in modern-day nativity scenes, then so Mary may have become suicidal. Along with the subsequent abandonment of the would-have-been father, the most celebrated Mother of all history may have become embittered & hopeless questioning the heavenly Father's unconditional love & acceptance of her very being. It's as though the Holiest of all women was forced to attend a figurative funeral procession for her only Child on the night of His birth; for once the Child is within the hands of the government, there is no guarantee of any return.

And the Child would be estranged & isolated in the fear of uncertainty & the grief of separation.

As one reflects upon the chorus of "Silent Night," one must take in the reality of life's chaos as children who are torn from their parent's arms are no longer able to "sleep in heavenly peace" while being sheltered in a stranger's house. Yet how often do self-righteous, self-acclaimed as dignified in character social workers, policemen, juvenile officers, & the CPS hot-lining neighbors take into effect this scenario?

Each of these may find a pew amongst their own family with children at their side proudly singing this refrain at Christmas time; yet how can it not bother their conscience to steal these children from the societal poor? With no remorse, the Church-inclined are causing their very own employee 'clients' to fall into absolute ruin as they wreak havoc upon them & their children.

No, Jesus didn't arrive to earth with an assembly of angels in a royal chariot born into a mansion or palace; nor did He find His way to earth crowned upon an empowered throne followed with a triumphant glow of the Sun's beaming as an infant. Jesus, a human Child born to us in a story of repeating abundance, was a baby who was saved from the disgrace of lofty thinking &

The Martyred Madonna

allowed to remain in the arms of His mother's care just as God intends for EACH of us who are gifted with the blessing of a child.

Although our children may not be the Savior of the World, the Prince of Peace, the King of Kings, many of them are still born into the same humble circumstance that this Christ of traditional remembrance was. The Child that each of us celebrates annually in birth should be the reminder of how EACH of our children born into poverty, humility, & the essence of ignobility should be offered the same honor. The honor of parenting – as God's nature has intended to allow the children to remain within the home of their biological, Heavenly gifting.

For God opens the womb & closes the womb. If God in His Omnipotent Being is wise enough to know where a child is best planted on earth, then God as the Author of Nature should be honored in allowing our children who are not endangered by actual negligence or violence to remain in the arms of their biological parents.

For each of those who disagree, they should ask God Himself WHY He allowed Jesus to come to earth in such lowly, human form. They should refrain from singing the verse "Away in A Manger" & replace the lyrics from 'Manger' to 'Mansion.' They should stifle in proclaiming their salvation in richness in their disbelief that God would love an individual who's poor. They should read the words that Jesus spoke before the disciples & the multitudes from Judea & Jerusalem,

> *"Blessed be ye poor; for ye shall be filled.*
> *Blessed are ye that weep now;*
> *For ye shall laugh . . . .*
>
> *. . . But woe unto you that are rich!*
> *For ye have received your consolation."*
>
> *Luke 6: 20, 21, . . . 24*

Yet despite Biblical warnings & reference to the cost of riches endangering salvation, there are the proud government officials who chose in modern day to intentionally cast curses upon the Silent Nights of children born into 'higher' societies.

Again, the Lamb of God would be rendered the crippled Lamb as an infant undeservedly punished with prolonged, unnecessary emotional & mental suffering.

& yet again, the Pharisees of society would be guilty even on the most celebrated day of history to be known for .... emotionally crippling children, robbing them of their childhood .... as they would the very Lamb of God.

English Lambchops =

So if one was to be faring through the dinner menu of the English social workers' climatic cafeteria, one would find as the main course of their delicacies to be "Lambchops" served as gourmet, sauce-fully seared, & spiced with financial bonus reward. Quite the grandeur grade of meat they choose for their diplomatic dinner of feasting. When one would assume that the children of choice for being intentionally 'kicked to the curb' of societal acceptance would be the least favored & the least desirable, even the most quality of breeding is chosen for the diplomatic dinners. While one would assume that 'grand-parenting' of the child would assist in any other familial concerns, the social service 'systemics' keep their bowel 'systems' plenty moving as they issue the abundance of children for the main course. Any questioning regarding the children's welfare in the hands of the government is considered 'absurd' for they are plentifully supplied to entertain, ascertain, & obtain with complete dining privileges upon them.

As all initiate in celebration with the clinking of
crystalline goblets, may the chorus verse begin:

"The Feast Is On"

"And now we gather here, to feast upon the throne,
of governmental guising, not one to dare as known;
the consequence – we have none, the beast of cruelty fares,
to skillfully, deceitfully partake the impoverished's heir.

For none found to defend them, it seems the course is known,
begins with recognition of their children safe at home;

but as we plan the menu, we find our glorious hand,
at solving economic woes, with feast of human lambs.

The feast is on, the feast is on, they've no one left to hide;
for we've partaken all our love & turned to greed's surmise.
The feast is on, the feast is on, & oer' the children's stare;
as 'fore we roast them, mindsets blur from pain that none's to care.
The feast is on, the feast is on, the children none to spare;
for all are found, a place within our celebration flair.

Yet as we watch & listen, between our bites of grand;
remaining child & mother, collapse in waning stance;
plead save their wailing children, screams the mother's praying hands,
yet our cannibal of instinct, is devouring hearts of lambs.

For though they strive to please us, it pleasures our demand,
of keeping up with progress, towards our feast of grand.
Though all are gripped with silence, in fear of governing throne,
so as they speak to mind us, our ears pleased to feed as foe.

The feast is on, the feast is on, they've no one left to hide;
for we've partaken all our greed, as perceived the guardian side.
The feast is on, the feast is on & oe'r the children's stare;
for when we roast them, they'll be scorned to death in mindset's 'care.'

The feast is on, the fest abounds, the children none to spare;
for all are found a place within our graveside feast of flair."

— *Elizabeth Heidelsen*

The Martyred Madonna

—The celebration of feast adjourns, until another harvest of lambs is scheduled.—

And so as the orderlies gather around, the lords & baronesses discuss the stately attributes of their lower courts yet few in recognition of the abominations of the social departments' causes of 'service.' The social departments upon visitation merely giggle & chort behind their desks – each appearing busied by an unseen agenda, not apparent as thieves of children's hearts, but merely 'social' as they'd be. For the social department is as such; they gather 'round & between their duties, chew their chocolates, feed their 'bubblies,' & hash the weather that be – making it seem as simple . . . simpletons as innocent beings. Yet inner prides & gloats of horror fill their mirrored minds. All is shining back from the visage of the inner amygdala to spot the devil's silver. That they seek – the devil's silver. The devilish silver appears to the other departments as a paycheck, a plop of pounds, a mere blindspot in the blinks of life. Yet to the socials & their assistive Bobbies, the devil's silver & the pleasure of inflicting pain is the spotlight. It's all a façade of a game persay . . . . yet not as one would know, the hidden agenda of seeking the devil's silver. For the devil's silver is merely too difficult for the cult-minded to resist with blaring, shining flashes under the glistening of the sun. The glistening has blinded their minds into automated fashion following the order's of their higher commands to pillage the children, fake mums' crimes, refrain from resolution, remain unsolved any reasonable equations to compromise, & sell off the majority of children that can be contained.

For containing is not an easy sort of ordeals, yet a guise of inconspicuous crafting. The aim is to maintain a low profile of the intention while over-glorifying the necessity to vilify the mum & proceed with orders to ignore optional distractions towards the end feast of lamb chops for devouring. For the children are dehumanized into a cannibal's course for the taking. In excuse, the socials will reason that the governing authorities, such as the final say of sorts, is in acceptance; therefore, they may continue our search throughout the Kingdom for delicacies of the kind – the littlest are their favorites. The more innocent & pure, the fresher the blood 'tis for tasting—as for momentary torment of pleasure.

And there it stands, the Feast that is rendered a necessity although in reality an abomination under the heavens . . . . For thy Kingdom come, thy will be done, on earth as it is in heaven. Never before has a loyal Kingdom-seeking soul silently witnessed, nor desired to devour, relinquish, or smear the reputation, being, & purity of a child in this Kingdom nor in the one to come. To do so, would gain one's place in the Feast of gnashing teeth & eternal weeping in return for their wickedness . . . . for the Kingdom of Heaven is 'such as these.'

In best recognition, to insist that one will not be a silent witness to the horrors that many departmental figures ensue is to please the heavenly Kingdom for the miracles of His ingenious creative engineering & architecture – the blessed purity of the child.

Shattering Hearts—

For in England, although many children are in actuality protected by the social services, there are those who become victims to this 'feasting' pattern; many programs are used for abuse by employees that 'assist' them. Yet concerning this 'human trafficking' & misfortune of the un-abused who become victimized, the hearts are not merely broken, but the faith, mind, & futuristic perspective are shattered. The English quite accurately refer to the disgusted practice as 'child farming;' the children are perceived as a mere production for the harvesting of the devil's silver. Although European human rights law states that children aren't to be sold, reportedly an approximate 54.2 million pounds per year are harvested through the English fostering agencies. Accordingly, an approximate 3 million pounds were utilized to train foster parents without recognition that there was an immediate set of grandparents willing & able to care for the suspected 'abused' children.

The social workers' job is most certainly to maintain this influx of readily available income; and as nature knows, there is always another child being birthed in a nearby hospital to maintain the supply of their hellacious demands. Accordingly, the managers take extreme measures to ensure that the children's parents are found to be ineffective; this challenge is obtained of 'guilty innocence' through intense pressure being placed upon the social workers to even re-write reports that appear too positive to be acceptable for their 'guilt files.'

In order to create these extensive 'guilt files,' the social workers must at all times maintain a persona of innocence in effort to disguise the ravenous wolf that hides beneath the wool of honorable public behavior.

Most oddly, once the socialite understands the pattern of presentable behavior & most easily sustains the image of pleasantry, the social wolves clothed in sheep's wool find the essence of distraction fundamentally the foundation for creating their files.

The 'guilt file' develops first from a 'look-out' employee most simply noted to be a bobby or even a friend of the social workers' office who makes an initial report or call to the child protection hotline. Most inconspicuously, the psychologists or counselors of the village are also on the 'look-out' for vulnerable mothers to prey upon. Once their target is found, the hunt begins. It starts with a direct line of fire seen as a pack of forest wolves released from their chamber—taking off into the woods, racing one after the other in the heat of primitive instinct to not only capture, but to kill. As one piles in behind the other, the wolves near closer to the innocent through perfected assembly. For once the lamb is reached in distant view, the wolves each separate in uniform distinction – one to the left, one to the right, in sets of two or three. Without breaking drive of drooling intent, the wolves' hunt is primitively uninterrupted & distinctively organized to production of entrapment. As each holds intimidating placement, the lamb's mother is the first removed; & then, the lamb himself remains in abandonment beckoning for his mother. Yet not one answers to the lamb's beckoning, inflicting severe emotional infliction upon the lamb. In exhausted attempts, the silence of the lamb instills intense fear upon his mindset in recognition that he is the next victim to the ravenous wolves that are lurking nearby on all sides in the woods.

Meanwhile, little to the innocent lamb's acknowledgement, the mother that was dragged away is being slowly devoured by the rest of the wolves' pack. This wolf pack is the critical 'team' that child protection services calls the 'family service team' in America—much simply abbreviated as FST in order to code the file. Other codes within American CPS files include P-referral which is the 'lookout' employee's initial case-producing hotline call. Here under the official coding, the children's biological parents are stoned with verbage & encrypted into a parental death trap.

The mocked witness to child abuse continues to snowball as one-by-one the wolves rip at another portion of the remaining carcass by each claiming the innocent parent labeled 'guilty;' although there is no evidence behind the claims of guilt, the onslaught continues to mercilessly tear at the living flesh of the usually remaining parent. The first parent is either incarcerated or thrown into regression due to fear based on violent physical threats & reputations made by enforcers of the governmental union – the local bobbies, bastardizing family, & the oppositional vengeful parent. Each of these 'members' of unified force becomes a significant stigma-producing challenge to the livelihood of the parent. Eventually, overflow into the parent's employment occurs; & in instances of vulnerability, the parent subsequently loses his or her job due to a significant decreased level of respect that occurs.

The ongoing call of the wolves to bleed the lambs of their dignity, respect, & many times their own lives is a heartless absurdity of lesser ranked governmental forces abusing the cause of legislative practice. Where legislative practice is aimed to protect & empower the citizen, the lesser ranking derive their authority of position to abuse, destroy, & negligently ignore the real reason of legislative enactment. With the cry of the wolves heard late in the night, as they thrive to find the next victim . . . . so too the lambs are still at risk of being devoured by these ravenous animals without the intervention of identifying, punishing, & halting these wolves from continuing in their abominable actions.

Results Verses Intentions:
Continued Failure of the Foster Care System

Failing statistics abound the foster care system despite the original intentions to protect children from their imagined or real 'parental predators.' According to the National Coalition for Child Protection Reform, an 80% failure occurs with the outcomes of foster care children; considering specifics, these foster care cases are individuals who have twice the rate of mental illness, double the rate of PTSD than Iraq war veterans, rendered 3 times as likely to be residing in poverty, & due to emotional/financial instability are 15 times less likely to be a college graduate.

Implications of foster home placement can either benefit the child in alleviating the stress of being neglected /abused or allow the child to become a 'placed' monetary asset. In the latter case, the child is abused through forced abandonment. One third of placements claim to have been abused by the parent or another residing adult in the foster home; however, abuse from severe emotional infliction & forced parental separation with denial of communication leave the child completely abandoned within a strange, new environment. At 18 years of age (when correlated Federal funding ceases), these foster children subsequently lose emotional & financial support. Thus, in reflection, the child that's evicted from their initial biological 'house' of residence is also many times being evicted from their 'home;' this biological 'home,' resembles their place of acceptance, comfort, & unconditional love. This denial of emotional support & approval is many times due to correlated funding. The biological parents' low income targets these families into intentional infliction of cruelty that authoritative figures of county seats render as justified. These children would obviously be more accepted with authority providing for their biological parents rather than for complete strangers to ensue parenting upon stigmatized 'foster children.'

Losing a biological parent can often times mean losing an entire family; I once heard a grandmother speak of her relationship to her biological grandson as being merely a 'foster parent & nothing else.' How cruel for family members to no longer accept their own relatives due to the stigma & embarrassment of forced welfare status.

In the State of Missouri in Greene County, several judges were asked to survey, examine, & recollect the reasoning, purpose, & outcome of a surplus of foster children who were placed into the CPS system. Greene County had apparently been selected for review due to the number of foster care children exceeding other Missouri counties by twice the amount. Through investigation of past files, the judges conveyed that the placements were identified as being justified by the juvenile court systems due to the lower economic familial status of the biological parents; and in disagreement, the judges stated that the children could have been better 'placed' in their own homes despite their parents' economic status.

Title VII of the Civil Rights Act of 1964 focuses upon employment as a significant area of concern rendering discrimination based on race, religion, sexual orientation, national origin, or color to be illegal; however, in legislation regarding civil rights, there is never once a reflection upon any ordinance governing the protection of families. When did employment – the accumulation of finances – become more important than maintaining, nurturing, & befriending your family? Can not the same simplistic application be offered through a Civil Rights Act allowing families to be protected by the same policy specifications? For instance, no family should be discriminated against for reasons of race, religion, sexual orientation, national origin, color, or economic status.

In collegiate discourse, a young West Indian woman compared American culture to her own past Caribbean heritage; in her opinion, she felt that America had placed greed above family & insinuated that family had been left behind in the mind of the American cultural conscience. Without application of life experiences & with solitary legislation for reference, America has evinced that racial discrimination in the area of education appears to be of radical significance. Countless Federal court cases on segregation such as *Sanford vs. Brown* have filled our law books, yet there remain the rights of the family to be protected.

Eviction notice? Many of us have never had to face an eight by ten letter taped to our door announcing that our humble temporary home is no longer available to us. Yet in Britain, there is official documentation which circulates throughout the neighborhoods of unfortunate citizens. These individuals are not allowed to return to their shelter at night with any peace of maintaining their most cherished relationship – that of their own children. For, as it reads, the 'children at your property are now at risk of becoming homeless' & 'a referral has been made to Children's Social Care.'

Many organizations in the United States have recognized the issues at hand & have channeled significant cause of concern into campaigns in their defense. One in particular is the Cradle to Prison Pipeline Campaign created by the Minnesota Child Defense program which is seeking to gain national attention to thousands of children who end up arrested, convicted, & incarcerated under judicial & legislative controls. These children, according to the Child Defense program, are 'funneled' down a ruinous pathway which ultimately traps them within the country in which they seek freedom.

And regarding costs, the issuance of countless children into the foster care programs of Minnesota has an average of $1,337 per child given to the respective foster parents under Title IV-E's allowance. Although this approximation appears to be a drop in the bucket, the cumulative affect of its payments have continued to deplete the United State's Social Security retirement fund from the Title IV-E division.

Until the American culture along with other more government-controlled countries decide to respect the rights of their families to raise their children in dignity & free from harassment, these 'structured' cultures will continue to decay at the basic foundational principles of familial establishment & equal rights. Striving for a higher quality of life will no longer be available for pursuit without an abolishment of government-protected civil rights denial. The single parent at the very least should be offered more support & respect when the other parent has abandoned their family.

Lost Lambs' Post-Separation Depression—

Post-partum depression for years has made headlines & news stories about famous celebrities & commoners being affected by the undesirable mental effect felt after the maternal birth of a child; however, far less recognized or acknowledged by the public media is the post-separation depression that much more profoundly affects not only the mind, but the actual biophysical model of the human body under the ultimate depressed reaction to loss of a child.

As one mother implicated, the loss of a child is in biological effect similar in reaction to the loss of one's limb. The medical challenges similarly exist with an initial shock reaction both mentally & physically with the body imploding in a fight or flight response. Tragically, in many cases, an increased chance of suicide is apparently correlated with the immediate loss of one's child.

In essence, this post-separation depression can be as much of a biological response in the maternal –child relationship severance than a mental one because the natural emotional attachment between the child & the mother is intensively strong. The key to factor in is that the separation is rendered under force completely against the mother's will. As seen with victims of the Auschwitz concentration camps under Hitler's regime, the familial separation under gunned, forced authority literally instigates a physical reactionary shock which debunks the foundational floor of past acknowledged acceptance & recognition as a worthy member of society. This societal betrayal of having a child permanently removed from one's life unexpectedly under ammunition-enforced legality essentially undermines the basic Maslow's hierarchy requirements for progressive living; for deliverance from safety is the basic foundational level of Maslow's pyramid which must be obtained before any rationalization can be rendered to relax in one's environment.

Ironically, one can be living at the height of Maslow's pyramid of potential & esteem when this unexpected turn proves that all of one's basic foundational thoughts are proven to be mere fallacies. For example, a mother's husband may be compelled by instinctive, primitive vengeance to rail a bout of accusations to the child protective hotline against her; & within a matter of days, the juvenile system has court ordered approval to remove her child without proof of actual abuse or neglect. The woman may then be turned on by police in effort to create a false criminal history all in the name of portraying the mother as unfit. The mother's sense of security which was previously stable & trusting has become a lost 'hierarchy' of which she now struggles at the bottom of its pyramid –resembling life itself. Unfortunately, the woman may take action in pleading with various resources only to find that all sense of attention in charity organizations such as domestic violence coalitions or parental rights committees all have no resources, no news contacts, & no advice for the 'unfit' mother. In reality, each of the mothers in a 'structured' society is vulnerable to be taken from the care of their biological parent without suspicion, recognition, or expectation made aware to them by authorities. Of course, this type of distressed circumstance in life is not encountered by everyone; therefore, the reality of relationships that individuals face in life should be addressed regarding those involving the 'harassment' relationships of government involvement which appear all too quickly.

There are basic required relationships that individuals deal with; some of these are chosen & others are forced upon them. It is the forced hostage state clearly in written law that is considered felonious under the realms of betraying another person's right to stay or leave as they choose. In the instance that a parent is placed under the suspicion of ill-parenting, the parent is forced by the juvenile court to remain within the area he or she resides in effort to complete ongoing requirements before reunification of the child to the parent is allowed. Although the parent may choose to leave & resist a relationship, the child is the dangling carrot that maintains the premise that the appropriate legal proceedings occur & that the parent(s) remain present as a coerced hostage.

"The Tears of Madonna: Adoption or Abduction?"

Back to encompassing the basic relationship dynamics approached in life, the biological self & other humans are two obvious relationships encountered; a third relationship can include one with a higher deity is relative to individual's religious perspective & understanding. There are, however, two other relationships that can be forced upon a citizen unexpectedly as mentioned previously – that of police-instigated legal authority revolving around alleged criminal activity & that of social work department investigation surrounding alleged juvenile endangerment.

Although these latter two forced relationships are both forms of governmental involvement, they are completely separate stress factors all together of sometimes incessant harassment. To the misfortune of the citizen who falls into the judgemental mistreatment of the courts, there is reason to emphasize this distinction because the level of stress amplifies itself if both areas are under investigation &/or on 'parole.'

If society were to aid the cause of humanity & the dignified treatment of human beings, news stories entitled 'Parents on Parole' would explicitly portray the effect of government involvement on the reputation & self—portrayal that one recognizes.

Although one is not entitled to government funding or assistance, basic humane treatment of fellow man should implicate that the basic love for one's own family as sisters & brethren within the same community should be a shared, unspoken given. Basic love for other community members would not only reach out to a misfortunate parent, but would also provide a reasonable amount of protection from government forces becoming over-involved & harassing a person's desire to parent a child. Immediate family being less supportive is still a real problem in today's society & needs to be addressed from a socio-cultural perspective.

Primitive ignorance remains at the core of the problem with civilized socialization being ignored. Primitive ignorance, for instance, rejects other family members on the mere reason that the individual is of unacceptable socioeconomic circumstance. Most obviously, children should be raised within a group of people openly expressing love amongst one another; however, the occurrence of a 'love-expressive' family is becoming more & more difficult to find. The more commonplace selfish pursuit of interests becomes & the more culturally conditioned that society is with being indifferent to family rejecting its own members for trivial reasons, the more segregated a country will become. For the lost lambs are not just lost to their own mothers, but lost to society many a time with homelessness, lack of acceptance from other societal members, & the stigma of rejection following not only through childhood, but through the remainder of their lives.

"One of the happiest days of my life, my proudest achievements, is giving birth and holding my newborn child. These women didn't have that experience. And I can't imagine it."—Senator Rachel Seiwert (overseer of the Senate Report Committee on forced adoptions in Australia)

Seiwert is referring to the forced adoptions of unwed mothers of which some were even held hostage in organized homes for up to 10 months while forced to await their child's abduction. Dan Rather who detailed this investigation in Australia interviewing over 100 women noted the absurdity of the occurrence in titling his news report "Adoption or Abduction?" Ironically, many American court-abducted children are stolen from the mothers & given to abusive fathers.

In contemplating the matters of forcing a child into the adoptive process, a distinct comparative end result occurs with the Madonna & modern victims of the SS. Just as these juvenile mothers are sent countless letters of notification regarding their child's case & repeatedly requested at court hearings & case meetings, the Holy Madonna spent hours awaiting her son's death as Jesus was trialed for the Crucifixion. These trialed women are given no mercy of recognition as prospective nurturing & providing parents. In the end, an expected & sometimes unexpected 'funeral' for the child to the Mother's care awaits many under the governmental officers' demanding. With intent of selfish cruelty, the mothers no longer are allowed to know of their child's whereabouts with completely severed communication accomplished through the governmental mission – a permanent obtaining of Termination of Parental Rights; in essence, respect towards the mother-child, 'Madonna' relationship is ignobly disgraced & abandoned to the Tomb of indifference & intentional cruelty forced upon humankind while the 'officials' take part in the Devil's silver.

"The Tears of Madonna"

She kneels again before the altar,
Knuckles bloodied scarlet;
In wailing, weeping visage,
'Oer agony she's forced to bear.

The Garden there upon us,
Greets her with no joy of splendor,
For the Child she bore has left her,
Under trial of burdened care.

In wails beyond the silence,
There's still none there left to hear her;
For the Governor & the Pulpit's backs,
Are turned with mocking jeer.

Empty heart left at the altar,
In withered stance of languish;
She turns with no relief,
'Oer all the pain she's suffered there.

The tears that fall are melting,
With the concrete of the silence;
The Devil's Silver stole away,
The Child she cried to spare.

The Martyred Madonna

Her garment drapes the floor,
With tread upon the Garden's stonesteps;
To find her way beyond,
Encumbered misery of care.

Unaware, within the Garden,
On softened soil Her tears have fallen,
There a miracle of splendor,
Grandeur lilies scattered there.

— Elizabeth Heidelsen

BIBLIOGRAPHY

Periodicals & Pamphlets:

"China's Brutal One-Child Policy," Jiang, Ma. *The New York Times*, May 21, 2013.

"*Number of Youth Aging Out of Foster Care Continues to Rise; Increasing 64 Percent Since 1999*," McCoy-Roth, Marci, Freundlich, Madelyn, Ross, Timothy. *Fostering Connections Resource Center* Analysis No.1, Jan 31, 2010.

"*Open Your Hearts To Life*!" *Respect Life* (1991) Confraternity of Christian Doctrine: Washington D.C. Secretariat of Pro-Life Activities, U.S. Conference of Catholic Bishops 3211 Fourth Street NE, Washington, DC 20017-1194. *www.usccb.org/prolife*

Books:

"Darkness Over Denmark," Levine, Ellen. NY, NY: Scholastic Inc., 2000 p. 23, 102, 118, 119.

"Depressed & Anxious," Marra, Thomas. Oakland, CA: New Harbinger Publications, Inc., 2004. p.121-122.

"Eichmann & the Holocaust," Arendt, Hannah. Ny, NY: The Penguin Group, 2006. p.32, 49, 51, 122.

"Luther & His Times," Schwiebert, E.G. St. Louis: Concordia, 1950. p. 750-752.

Elizabeth Heidelsen

"*Pouch*," Stein, David, Ezra. www.davidezra.com

"*Schindler's Legacy*" Brecher.Elinor. Ny, NY: Penguin Group, 1994. p. xxii, 432.

<u>Websites</u>:

www.bbc.co.uk/news/uk-24798498
www.casaforchildren.org
www.charlesstangor.com/2012/movenos
www.childdefense.txt
www.childrenscreamingtobeheard.com
www.childrenunitingnations.org
<u>www.cwla.org/programs/fostercare/factsheet.htm</u> "Quick Facts About Foster Care."
www.divorcecorps.com
<u>www.gingerbreadman.com</u> . . . .
<u>www.historacle.org/hitlers_supermen.html</u>
www.jewishvirtuallibrary.org/source/Holocaust/Lebensborn.html
www.livescience.com/27400-kangaroos.html
www.loveandlogic.com
<u>www.lucifereffect.com</u>
www.merriamwebsterdictionary . . . .
<u>www.nrcpfc.org/fostering_connections</u>
<u>www.stoptheabusecampaign.com</u>
www.topconservativeness.com/cdc-whites
<u>www.yahoonews.com</u> "Adopted or Abducted?" Rather, Dan (March 27, 2012).
http://speye.files.wordpress.com/2013/11/kht-threat-letter-socil-services.jpg

www.ingramcontent.com/pod-product-compliance
Lightning Source LLC
Chambersburg PA
CBHW021025180526
45163CB00005B/2115